Usborne

History of the World in 100 Pictures

Rob Lloyd Jones

Illustrated by Galia Bernstein

Designed by Tom Lalonde and Samantha Barrett

History consultant: Dr. Anne Millard

by 18,000BC* — First people

10,000BC — First farmers

3500BC — First wheels

3500BC — City of Ur

1 The first people

Cave paintings from Lascaux, France

This painting, showing two bison, was discovered on the wall of a **cave in Lascaux**, in the south of France. It was made around 20,000 years ago, by some of the the **first people** to move from place to place to hunt animals to eat. They painted pictures of the animals they hunted on cave walls using paint made from ground-up minerals.

Ancient Times

The first people hunted animals, and learned to grow crops. Then, around 5,000 years ago, the first civilizations grew up...

2 The first farmers

This **decorated pot** was used by one of the earliest farmers, to store grain. **Farming** began in the Middle East around 12,000 years ago, when people learned how to grow crops. Now that they didn't have to move around to find food, they settled down in one place.

3 The first wheels

This panel covered in **mosaics from Sumer** (now Iraq) is one of the oldest scenes showing **wheels**. Wheels were first used by armies in Sumer, around 5,500 years ago, to build the first chariots.

* 'BC' means 'Before Christ'. BC dates are counted backwards after the birth of Jesus Christ (in the year 0).

18,000BC - 2000BC

3500BC First writing — 2686BC Egyptian Old Kingdom — 2000BC Mohenjo-daro

4 The city of Ur

Royal helmet from Ur

This **golden helmet** was probably worn by a Sumerian king in **Ur**, one of the world's first cities. The **first cities** grew up in Sumer around 3500BC, as farming villages grew into towns, and then got even bigger. Ur had mud-brick houses, schools and temples.

5 The first writing

Around 3500BC, the world's earliest writing developed in both Egypt and Sumer, to keep records of who owned what. This **fragment from a wall decoration** is painted with picture signs from the Egyptian script, **hieroglyphics** (meaning 'sacred writing').

6 Egyptian Old Kingdom

This carved **makeup palette** (plate) shows a king called Menes, who became the first king to rule all of Egypt, around 2900BC.

Egyptian makeup palette

From around 2686BC, Egypt entered a period known as the **Old Kingdom**, when pyramids were built as tombs for powerful kings.

7 Mohenjo-daro, Indus Valley

This statue probably shows a priest or ruler from **Mohenjo-daro**, one of the first great cities in the **Indus Valley** (now in Pakistan). The stone figure, carved around 2000BC, wears a headband and patterned robe, to show his important status in society.

Stone figure from Mohenjo-daro

1900BC Minoans — from 1650BC Hittites — 1500BC Egyptian New Kingdom — 800BC Assyrian Empire

8 The Minoans

Mural from Knossos, Crete

This **painted mural**, showing a man leaping over a charging bull, decorated the wall of a spectacular palace at **Knossos**, on the Mediterranean island of Crete. The palace was built by people from one of Europe's first great civilizations, the **Minoans**, who ruled Crete from around 1900Bc to 1450BC. Bull-leaping like this might have been part of a ceremony held at the palace.

9 The Hittites

This **silver drinking cup** was made by people called **Hittites**, who ruled most of Turkey and Syria, from around 1650BC to 1180BC. Hittites believed the natural world was full of divine spirits. This vessel was probably made as an offering to spirits that lived in stags.

Hittite drinking vessel

10 The Egyptian New Kingdom

This gold **death mask** was found on the body of Egyptian king **Tutankhamun**, which lay among hundreds of treasures in his tomb. From around 1500BC, a time in Egyptian history known as the **New Kingdom** kings were buried in tombs cut into the rocks of a sacred valley near their capital Thebes.

Death mask of Tutankamun

11 The Assyrian Empire

Statue from Nineveh

Around 800BC, rulers from Assyria conquered lands across the Middle East. This collossal statue of a **winged lion** with the head of a king stood at the entrance to the palace of **Ashurnasirpal II**, an Assyrian king who built grand palaces and temples at his capital **Nineveh**.

1900BC - 600BC

800BC Olmecs

600BC Start of Buddhism

600BC City of Babylon

12 The Olmecs, Central America

This **massive stone head** (about 3m, or 10ft, high) was carved by one of the earliest civilizations in Central America - the **Olmecs**. It is probably the face of a ruler, and was found at a site called San Lorenzo, where the Olmecs built temples to their gods.

Olmec head, San Lorenzo

13 The start of Buddhism

This painting from Tibet shows a scene from the life of an Indian prince named **Siddhartha Gautama** who, around 600BC, gave up his wealth and became a holy man. Known as '**the Buddha**' ('the enlightened one'), his ideas formed the basis of the religion **Buddhism**.

Painting of the Buddha from Tibet

Panel from the Ishtar Gate

14 The city of Babylon

This **golden dragon** is one of 120 creatures that adorned the **Ishtar Gate**, the entrance to the city of Babylon, in around 600BC. Beyond the gate rose a towering **ziggurat**, or temple, and a lavish building with waterfalls and hanging plants, known as the '**Hanging Gardens of Babylon**'.

500BC to 338BC
The Classical Period in Greece

480BC
Battle of Thermopylae

15 The Classical Period, Greece

This vase, decorated with scenes of ***Ancient Greek*** soldiers, was made in Athens during a time of Greek history known as the **Classical Period,** from 500Bc to 338BC. This was the great age of '**city states**', which were often at war with each other. Athens was by far the most powerful city state. It had the first '**democratic**' government (all free men could vote), and was home to Greece's finest artists.

Painted vase from Athens

16 The Battle of Thermopylae

This statue shows **Leonidas**, a military leader from the Greek state of **Sparta**. In 480BC, around 100,000 soldiers from Persia (now Iran) attacked Greece. It was left to Leonidas and 300 Spartans to fight back, at a narrow pass called **Thermopylae**. Although they were defeated, the Spartans inspired the rest of Greece to drive off the invaders.

Statue of Spartan king Leonidas

Fragment of mosaic scene showing Alexander the Great

17 Alexander the Great

In 336BC, all of Greece was conquered by King Philip II of Macedonia. His son ***Alexander*** (336BC-323BC) conquered lands as far as India, and became known as 'Alexander the Great'. This **mosaic scene,** from the floor of a Roman villa, shows Alexander riding his horse, Bucephalus, into battle.

336BC-323BC Alexander the Great

221BC First Emperor of China

200BC Celts

by 100BC Roman Empire

Year 29 Crucifixion of Jesus

A 'Terracotta Warrior' from China

18 The First Emperor, China

This statue made from a type of pottery called terracotta is one of **8,000 life-sized models of soldiers** buried in 210BC with Chinese ruler **Qin Shi Huangdi**, to serve him in the 'next life'. Qin Shi Huangdi was the first ruler to unite all of China, and he called himself the '**First Emperor**'.

19 Celtic tribes

This **bronze shield** was found in the River Thames, in London. It was thrown into the river around 2,200 years ago as a gift to gods by people called **Celts**. The Celts lived in tribes across Europe. They were often at war with each other, but they all shared a similar language and way of life.

20 The Roman Empire

By the end of the 1st century BC, the **Romans** had conquered lands all around the Mediterranean Sea. The **Roman army** was one of the best-trained in the world. Its soldiers, known as legionaires, wore **bronze helmets** like this one into battle.

Roman legionaire's helmet

Icon showing the crucifixion of Jesus

21 The crucifixion of Jesus

This **religious painting**, or **icon**, shows the execution by crucifixion (being fixed to a cross) of a man named **Jesus**, in Jerusalem around the year 29. Jesus was hailed by his followers as the son of God. They called him Jesus Christ and spread his teachings, and a new religion emerged, called **Christianity**.

The city of Byzantium, around the year 600

The Middle Ages

From around the year 400, new empires and religions rose up around the world, inspiring craftspeople to create stunning works of art.

22 The Han dynasty

In 202BC, a soldier named Liu Bang became the first emperor of the **Han dynasty**, which ruled China for the next 400 years - a time of great wealth, when craftspeople made beautiful objects. This **bronze lantern was** found in a noble lady's tomb in China, alongside a body encased in dazzling jade.

Han dynasty bronze lantern

23 The Byzantine Empire

Byzantine mosaic showing Justinian

By about the year 400, the **Roman Empire** had split into two parts: east and west. This glittering **mosaic** shows **Justinian** (in the middle), who ruled the eastern part, known as the **Byzantine Empire**, from 527. He captured new lands, where he had churches built and decorated with intricate mosaics.

24 The Silk Road

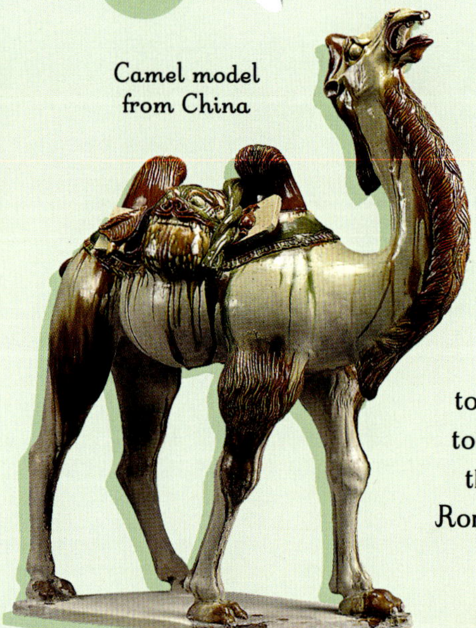

Camel model from China

This **Chinese model** shows a camel loaded with goods, about to set off along the **Silk Road** - an overland trade route that led from China to Europe over 6,400km (around 4,000 miles). From around 200 to 1450, Chinese merchants took silk and spices along this route, to trade with Romans for gold and slaves.

202BC - 750

from 202BC
Han dynasty

by 400
Byzantine Empire

25 The Maya

This **stone plaque** was made to celebrate a religious festival by a Mayan tribe, who lived in the rainforests of Central America between around 250 and 900. The **Maya** built spectacular stone cities, with pyramid temples where they sacrificed prisoners of war to their gods.

Mayan stone plaque

Koran from Morocco

26 The start of Islam

From 610, a new religion – **Islam** – spread across the Middle East, based on the teachings of a man named **Mohammad**. Mohammad's followers wrote down his messages in a holy book called the **Koran**. This Koran, from Morocco, is decorated with gold leaf and decorative Arabic script.

27 The Abbasid Empire

By 750, a family called the **Abbasids** became **caliphs**, or rulers, of the **Islamic world**. From their magnificent capital, **Baghdad**, they encouraged traders to set off on journeys to far-off lands. This painting shows Muslim merchants riding **camels on a trading expedition**.

711 - 800

711
Moors in Spain

by around 750
Illuminated manuscripts

28 The Moors, Spain

This **ivory jar**, from **Southern Spain**, was used for Christian ceremonies, but is decorated with Arabic script and patterns. In 711, most of Spain came under the control of **Muslim rulers known as Moors**, and remained so for over 700 years. Christian communities in Spain gradually adopted parts of Islamic culture.

Ivory jar from Southern Spain

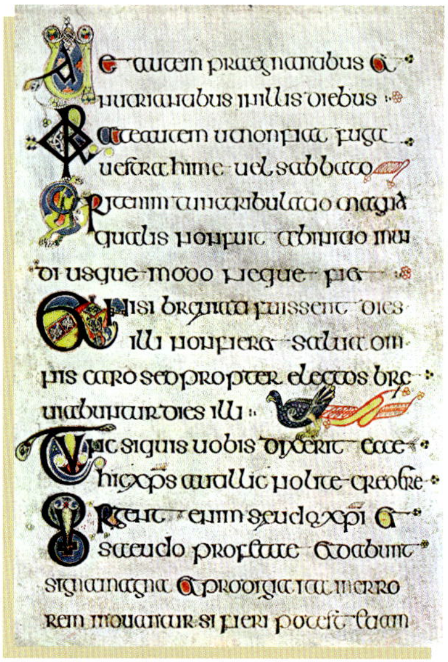
Ve autem praegnantibus et
nutrientibus in illis diebus
Orate autem ut non fiat fuga
vestra hieme vel sabbato
Erit enim tunc tribulatio magna
qualis non fuit ab initio mun
di usque modo neque fiet
Et nisi breviati fuissent dies
illi non fieret salva om
nis caro sed propter electos bre
viabuntur dies illi
Tunc si quis vobis dixerit ecce
hic xps aut illic nolite credere
Surgent enim pseudo xpi et
pseudo profetae et dabunt
signa magna et prodigia ita ut in erro
rem moveantur si fieri potest etiam

Page from the Book of Kells

29 Illuminated manuscripts

This page is from the **Book of Kells**, a collection of Bible stories handwritten in a monastery in Ireland around the year 800. In Europe, Christian monks and nuns lived apart from the world, in **monasteries** and **nunneries**. They prayed, treated the sick, and made decorated books like this one, known as '**illuminated manuscripts**'.

30 The Maori, New Zealand

Around 750, a tribe called the **Maori** sailed from islands in the Pacific Ocean to **New Zealand**, where they settled. Many Maori wore **greenstone charms** called '**hei-tiki**', like this one, on necklaces. The hei-tiki were sacred symbols, which the Maori believed gave them good luck.

Carved figure from a Viking longship

31 The Vikings

This **carved dragon figure** decorated the front of a **Viking** ship, known as a **longship**. Vikings were warriors and farmers from Sweden, Norway and Denmark. By 790, they began to leave their homelands and search for new territory. For the next 300 years, they raided villages around the coasts of Europe.

750
Maori reach New Zealand

790
Viking raids begin

800
Charlemagne becomes emperor

by 800
Spread of Hinduism

from 800
Khmer dynasty

32 Charlemagne

This scene shows the Pope crowning King Charles as '**Emperor of the Romans**', on Christmas Day of the year 800. Charles had become king of most of France in 768, and over the next 30 years he built a **Christian empire** across Europe. He became known as Charles the Great - or **Charlemagne**.

33 Spread of Hinduism

This **sculpture, from a temple in Orissa**, India, shows a god called Surya, from the Hindu religion. By around 800, **Hinduism** had spread across most of India. Hindus worshipped in beautifully decorated temples, dedicated to their many gods.

Sculpture from Orissa

34 The Khmer dynasty

Sculpture from Angkor

By the 800s, several kingdoms in Southeast Asia had grown powerful, influenced by Hindu or Buddhist kingdoms in India. The greatest was ruled by the **Khmer dynasty**, from their spectacular capital Angkor (now in Cambodia). Around half a million people lived there, among palaces and temples to Hindu gods. This **sculpture from Angkor** shows a fierce creature that guarded a temple.

The largest temple at Angkor - **Angkor Wat** - was originally dedicated to the Hindu god Vishnu.

Section of the Bayeux Tapestry

35 The Battle of Hastings

This scene is from the **Bayeux Tapestry**, a 70m (230ft) embroidered cloth that tells the story of the victory of Duke William of Normandy over King Harold of England at the **Battle of Hastings**, in 1066. William took the English crown and ruled as '**William the Conqueror**'.

36 Kingdom of Ife

This **bronze head** shows a ruler of the **Kingdom of Ife**, in West Africa. By around 1100, Ife - as well as other kingdoms in **West Africa** - had grown rich from trading with Arab merchants. The people of Ife were expert metalworkers, who developed new ways of working with bronze.

Bronze head from Ife

37 The Crusades

In 1095, the Pope (the head of the Catholic Church) called for European knights to reclaim Jerusalem from Muslim control. This sparked '**the Crusades**' - a series of wars against Muslim rulers over 200 years. This **illuminated manuscript** shows Crusader knights clashing with Muslim warriors in battle.

38 Samurai, Japan

Japanese painting of a samurai

In 1192, a powerful noble named **Minamoto Yoritomo** became the first **shogun**, or military commander, of Japan. His army was made up of highly trained warriors called **samurai**. Dressed in elaborately decorated suits, samurai were trained to win or die, and never surrender. This **Japanese painting** shows a samurai attacking on horseback, with a bow and arrow.

- 1066 Battle of Hastings
- 1095 The Crusades begin
- by 1100 Kingdom of Ife
- 1192 Minamoto Yoritomo becomes shogun
- 1186 Saladin unites the Islamic Middle East

39 Saladin

Portrait of Saladin

By 1186, one Muslim ruler had united the Islamic cities of the Middle East. Skilled military leader **Salah al-Din** (also known as **Saladin**) then defeated many Crusaders, European knights with kingdoms in the Middle East, and re-captured Jerusalem. This portrait of Saladin was painted around 1180.

40 Genghis Khan

This scene, from 1206, shows a warrior named Temujin being named ruler of the ***Mongols*** - nomadic tribes of Central Asia - and given the name **Genghis Khan,** meaning 'supreme ruler'.

Under Genghis Khan, and later his sons, the Mongols captured new lands from China to Eastern Europe, slaughtering anyone who dared to resist. Their empire lasted until 1300.

41 Magna Carta

Copy of the Magna Carta

In 1215, a group of English nobles, or barons, forced **King John** to sign the '***Magna Carta***' (Great Charter). This document stated that the King should talk to a council of barons and bishops before making big decisions. The first council - known as '**Parliament**' - was held in 1275. The idea soon spread across Europe, as a way of keeping check on royal power.

Genghis Khan lived in a yurt (tent) that was pulled on wheels as he moved from battle to battle.

1066 - 1215

1206 Genghis Khan becomes Mongol ruler

1215 Magna Carta

by 1200 European cathedrals

1271 Travels of Marco Polo

1300 Easter Island

1347 Black Death reaches Europe

42 European cathedrals

By the year 1200, Europe entered a golden age of **cathedral building**. Huge new churches were built, decorated with statues, carvings and dazzling **stained glass windows**. Most people couldn't read, so the windows were used to tell stories from the Bible.

This window, from **Chartres Cathedral** in France, shows Jesus' last supper with his disciples, or followers.

43 The Travels of Marco Polo

This **medieval manuscript** shows a merchant named **Marco Polo** arriving at the city of Hormuz in Persia (now Iran). Marco Polo set off from Venice in the year 1271, on a 20 year journey around Asia. His stories were recorded in one of the first travel books, **'The Travels of Marco Polo'**, introducing people from Europe to cultures of the East.

44 Easter Island

This huge **stone statue** is one of around 900 similar sculptures carved by the people of **Easter Island** in the Pacific by around 1300. The statues – some of which are over 12m (40ft) tall – stood on platforms around the island's coast, and were probably meant to represent powerful island chiefs.

Stone statue from Easter Island

1200 - 1455

by 1350 Great Zimbabwe at its height

1368 Ming dynasty beings

1455 Printing press

Engraving of Black Death victims

45 The Black Death

In 1347, a deadly disease reached Europe from Asia, carried by fleas that lived on rats. Victims were covered in black swellings that gave the plague its name - the **Black Death**. The Black Death ravaged Europe for six years, killing at least one in every three people.

46 Great Zimbabwe

This **soapstone figure** was found at the site of **Great Zimbabwe**, in Southern Africa. By around 1350, Great Zimbabwe had grown into a wealthy trading base. Its rulers lived inside a walled fortress in a city of around 20,000 people.

Soapstone figure from Great Zimbabwe

47 Ming dynasty, China

Ming dynasty vase

In 1368, the **Ming dynasty** took control of China. The Ming emperors ruled for the next 280 years, and built a lavish palace complex in Beijing, known as the '**Forbidden City**'. Chinese art flourished during this period. Vases like this one, made of **blue and white porcelain**, became prized throughout the world.

48 Invention of the printing press

This **Bible** is one of the **first books printed in Europe**. Until the 1450s, books had to be copied out by hand, so were very expensive. Then, in 1455, a German named **Johannes Gutenberg** printed this Bible using a machine called a **printing press**, which printed one page at a time. Now, books could be made quickly and cheaply. Soon there were printing presses all over Europe.

The Gutenberg Bible

from 1350 The Renaissance — 1492 Christopher Columbus — from 1517 The Reformation — 1500s Aztecs

49 The Renaissance

'Crouching Boy' by Michelangelo

From 1350, artists in Italy began to try out new ideas inspired by the art and learning of Ancient Greece and Rome. This movement, known as the **Renaissance**, or 'rebirth', reached its height in the 1500s, with the work of artists such as **Leonardo da Vinci**, and **Michelangelo** – who carved this lifelike **statue of a crouching boy**.

50 The European Reformation

This painting shows **Martin Luther**, a German monk who, in 1517, wrote a list of 95 ways that the Catholic Church could be reformed. His ideas began a movement called the **Reformation**, as people broke away from the Church and formed new '**Protestant**' churches. Over the next 100 years, Protestant and Catholic nations fought each other all over Europe.

Portrait of Martin Luther

Age of Discovery

The 16th and 17th centuries were a time of great change, as European explorers discovered previously unknown lands, and new ideas developed in science and art.

51 Christopher Columbus

This is a model of the ***Santa Maria***, the ship that Italian captain **Christopher Columbus** sailed when he reached the West Indies in 1492. Later, in 1519, Portuguese explorer ***Ferdinand Magellan*** led the first expedition to sail all the way around the world.

Model of the *Santa Maria*

1500s Ottoman Empire — 1500s Kingdom of Benin — 1500s Incas

52 The Aztecs

Aztec snake pendant

This **two-headed serpent**, made from wood and turquoise, may have been worn as a pendant by an Aztec priest. The **Aztecs** were a warlike people who ruled over a large part of Mexico by around 1500. As well as being warriors, the Aztecs were also skilled craftsmen.

53 The Ottoman Empire

This **crown** of gold and jewles belonged to an **Ottoman** ruler, or **sultan**, called **Suleiman the Magnificent** (1520-1566). From their luxurious Topkapi Palace, in Istanbul, the Ottoman Turks ruled a vast empire around the Mediterranean Sea. Their power was a huge threat to European rulers.

Ottoman royal crown

Bronze plaque from Benin

54 The Kingdom of Benin

By around 1500 in West Africa, the **Kingdom of Benin** had grown rich from trading slaves with Portuguese merchants. Its ruler (called an **oba**) lived in an enormous palace with pillars decorated with **bronze plaques**, like this one showing important army chiefs.

55 The Inca

Gold disc showing the Inca sun god

By 1500, the **Inca** people had built a powerful empire in Peru, conquering land along the Pacific coast and the Andes mountains. They built stunning stone cities, such as **Machu Picchu**. This **gold disc** shows the Inca sun god *Inti*, who was worshipped in temples across the Empire.

Around 1,000 people lived in the Inca city of Machu Picchu.

56 Emperor Charles V

Painting of Charles V

From the end of the 1400s, after clever marriages and alliances, the powerful **Hapsburg family**, from Austria, had built up an empire in Europe. This painting shows Hapsburg emperor **Charles V**. He came to power in 1519, and increased the size of the empire even further by winning wars against France and the Ottomans.

The Taj Mahal, in Agra, India

57 The Mughals

This **jade dagger handle**, inlaid with jewels, was made by craftsman from the Mughal empire in India. The **Mughals**, a Muslim dynasty from Afghanistan, ruled India from 1526. They built mosques, forts and palaces, but their most famous monument was the **Taj Mahal** – a huge marble tomb for the wife of Emperor Shah Jahan.

Mogul dagger handle

58 Nicolaus Copernicus

In the Middle Ages, most people believed that the Sun went around Earth. In 1543, Polish astronomer **Nicolaus Copernicus** claimed that the Earth orbited the Sun. His ideas formed the basis of modern astronomy. This engraving shows his new **model of the universe**, with the Sun in the middle.

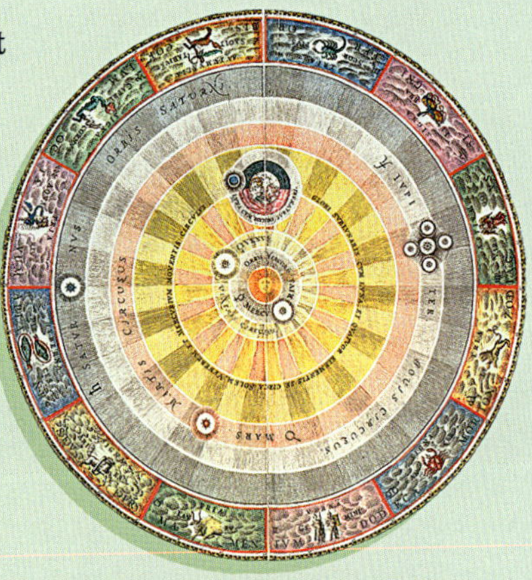

Copernicus's model of the universe

59 The Spanish Armada

This painting shows an attempted invasion of England, in 1588, by a fleet of ships known as the **Spanish Armada**. King Philip II of Spain had hoped to overthrow Elizabeth I of England, but the attack was a disaster. The Spanish lost the battle, and many of their ships were wrecked in a storm.

1519 Charles V

from 1526 Mughals in India

1543 Copernicus

1588 Spanish Armada

from 1613 Romanov dynasty in Russia

60 The Romanovs

In 1613, a new family of rulers called the **Romanovs** took control of Russia. Under their greatest rulers Peter the Great (1682-1725) and Catherine the Great (1762-1796), Russia grew into one of the strongest countries in Europe. The **Imperial Crown of Russia**, shown here, was used to crown Russian tsars, or emperors, from 1762 to 1917.

The Imperial Crown of Russia

A scene from Romeo and Juliet

61 William Shakespeare

Mr. WILLIAM
SHAKESPEARES
COMEDIES,
HISTORIES, &
TRAGEDIES.
Publifhed according to the True Originall Copies.

Portrait of William Shakespeare

The reign of **Queen Elizabeth I** (1558-1603), was a **golden age** for the arts in England. In London, thousands crammed into new playhouses, such as the *Globe*. The best known playwright was **William Shakespeare**, whose plays such as *Hamlet* and *Romeo and Juliet* are still performed all over the world.

62 The Pilgrims

This painting shows a group known as the **Pilgrims**, about to set off from England, on a voyage to America, in August 1620. They set up one of the first successful colonies on the east coast of North America, at a place they called **Plymouth**. Soon, more and more settlers sailed from Europe, seeking new lives in what became known as the 'New World'.

Carving of Louis XIV

63 The Sun King

This golden carving, from the gates of the **Palace of Versailles**, near Paris, France, shows **Louis XIV** (1643-1715), also known as the Sun King, who built the palace, and was the most powerful ruler in Europe at the time. Louis ordered his nobles to live at the palace with him, but refused to consult them on important issues, believing he had absolute power given to him from God.

64 The Age of Enlightenment

Isaac Newton's orrery

This **orrery, a model of the Solar System**, belonged to **Isaac Newton**, an English physicist who, discovered **how gravity works** in the 1660s. The next 100 years in Europe was a time when fresh discoveries were made in science, and new ideas emerged about society and religion. It's known as the '**Age of Enlightenment**'.

65 Baroque music

By 1700 a new style of music, known as '**Baroque**', was popular in Europe, with well known **composers** such as Bach, Handel and Vivaldi. Exquisite new instruments were made, such as this viola carved by **Antonio Stradivari**, an Italian master craftsman.

Viola carved by Stradivari

1700s Baroque music

1768-1779 Voyages of Captain Cook

1776 Declaration of Independence

1789 French Revolution

66 Voyages of Captain Cook

This painting shows **Captain James Cook** landing in Australia in 1770, and claiming the country for Britain. In 1768, Cook set out from Britain to explore the islands of the South Pacific. Over three voyages, he and his crew mapped several islands, including the coast of New Zealand.

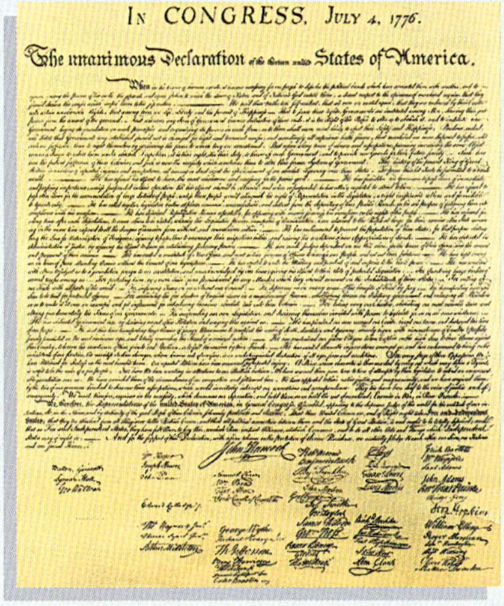
IN CONGRESS, JULY 4, 1776.

The unanimous Declaration of the thirteen united States of America.

The Declaration of Independence

67 The Declaration of Independence

By the 1700s, Britain had 13 colonies on the east coast of North America. But settlers there grew angry at heavy taxes and strict laws imposed by the British government. In 1776, leaders from the colonies signed this document, the **Declaration of Independence**, stating they were an independent country, which they called the **United States of America**.

68 The French Revolution

From 1789, a **revolution** broke out in France. Furious at high taxes, working people overthrew the government. **Guillotines** (machines, like this one, that chopped off people's heads) became a symbol of freedom, as the King and thousands of nobles were dragged to their deaths.

69 Napoleon Bonaparte

In 1799, army general **Napoleon Bonaparte** seized control of France, determined to build an empire. By 1812, he had conquered most of Western Europe, but his invasion of Russia was a disaster, as thousands of French soldiers died in freezing snow. In 1815, Napoleon was finally defeated by British and Prussian armies at the **Battle of Waterloo**.

Painting of Napoleon Bonaparte

70 The British in India

Arms of the British East India Company

This is the arms of the **British East India Company**, a trading company that governed large parts of India from 1757. After Indian soldiers rebelled against the Company in 1857, the **British government** took control of India, and ruled until 1947.

Empires and Inventions

The 18th and 19th centuries saw empires rise and fall, nations fight for independence, and staggering inventions that changed the world.

71 The Industrial Revolution

By the 1800s, new inventions were changing how people lived and worked, leading to an '**Industrial Revolution**' all over the world. **Steam powered machines** did jobs, such as spinning cloth, that had previously been done by hand. **Steam trains** allowed goods to be transported over long distances for the first time. This is a replica of **one of the first trains, *The Rocket***, designed by George Stephenson in 1804.

1757-1947 British in India

1799 Napoleon Bonaparte comes to power

1800s Industrial Revolution

The Order of the Liberator

72 Independence in South America

This medal, known as the **Order of the Liberator**, commemorates the Venezuelan commander **Simon Bolivar**, who freed much of South America from Spanish rule. Bolivar and his army drove Spanish troops from New Granada (Colombia), Venezuela, Ecuador and Peru. Part of Peru became a new nation, named after him – Bolivia. By 1830 all of South America was free from European rule.

73 Abolition of slavery

Since the 1500s, millions of people from Africa had been forced onto ships and sent to the Americas to work as **slaves**. By the 1800s, though, many people in Europe wanted to end the inhuman slave trade. This pendant, with the question, 'Am I not a man and a brother?' became a symbol for the **movement to end slavery**. In 1833, it was finally **abolished** in the British Empire, and in 1865 it became illegal in North America.

74 The first 'computer'

This is a replica of a machine designed by English mathematician **Charles Babbage** in 1834. Called an '**Analytical Engine**', it was the first machine that could be programmed to make calculations, and store information. Although he never built it, Babbage is thought to have designed the world's **first computer**.

Replica of Babbage's Analytical Engine.

75 The first photographs

This camera, known as a '**Daguerreotype**' was invented in 1839 by French painter and physicist **Louis Daguerre**, to create the **first photographs**. New technologies and techniques later made photography more practical, but Daguerre is remembered as the 'father of photography'.

A Daguerreotype camera

Portrtai of Giuseppe Garibaldi

76 The rise of nations

In 1829, **Greece** became independent of the Ottoman Empire, and one year later **Belgium** won independence from the Netherlands. In 1861 the **Italian states** joined to form one nation, after a rebellion by a freedom fighter named **Giuseppe Garibaldi** (shown here). In 1871, **Germany** was united, too, under King Wilhelm I.

77 Charles Darwin and evolution

This armadillo was collected by English naturalist **Charles Darwin,** in Argentina in 1833. Twenty six years later, in 1859, he published a book - '**On the Origin of Species by Means of Natural Selection**' - based on his studies of animals and plants, and proposing a new theory about how they had evolved over time. Darwin's theory is still accepted by most scientists today.

Armadillo collected by Darwin

78 The Communist Manifesto

Statue of Karl Marx and Friedrich Engels

This statue shows **German thinkers Karl Marx** and **Friedrich Engels.** In 1848 they published a book called '**The Communist Manifesto**', urging workers around the world to unite to gain more power over their bosses and rulers. Its ideas influenced the development of **communism** - a system of government that played a huge part in world politics in the 20th century.

from 1829
Rise of nations

1848
Communist Manifesto

1859
Charles Darwin publishes 'On the origin of species'

79 The American Civil War

Union battle drum

From 1861, the USA was torn apart by a four year war, as '**Union**' forces of the northern states tried to stop the '**Confederate**' southern states from breaking away and forming their own nation. The Union eventually won the **American Civil War**, and the USA emerged as a single nation. This **battle drum** was used by the Union army. By using different drum beats, drummers could send signals between officers and troops.

80 Invention of the telephone

In March 1876, Scottish inventor **Alexander Graham Bell** used this device - **the first telephone** - to transmit sound using electricity. The first sentence Bell spoke through the telephone was to his assistant Thomas Watson - "Mr. Watson, come here, I want you."

The first telephone

British soldiers clashing with Zulu warriors at the Battle of Isandlwana, in 1879

81 The Anglo-Zulu War

This painting shows a battle between **British soldiers** and **Zulu warriors,** in southern Africa. During the 1800s, Africa became a battleground for European nations competing to gain land, and many native Africans fought back. In 1879, Zulus armed with spears and shields fought against British troops, but they were defeated - and more and more European nations joined what became known as the **Scramble for Africa**.

1861 American Civil War

1829 - 1879

1876 First telephone

1879 Anglo-Zulu War

1879 - 1912

Replica of Edison's incandescent lamp

82 Invention of light bulbs

This is a replica of an **incandescent lamp** – the **first practical light bulb**, invented in 1879 by American **Thomas Edison**. By then, several scientists had experimented with electricity to make light, but Edison's invention was the first to use a carbon 'filament' inside a glass bulb, to create a long-lasting glow.

83 The first car

In 1885, German engineer **Karl Benz** built the first 'automobile' to be powered by an **internal combustion engine**. Although there had been other automobiles before, they had been run on steam or electricity. Benz's invention (called the **Benz Patent-Motorwagen**) is regarded as the **world's first car**.

The Benz Patent-Motorwagen

Sioux tribe tunic

84 The Massacre at Wounded Knee

This tunic was worn by a member of the **Sioux**. They were one of the **Native American tribes** who fought to keep their homeland, as more and more of it was seized by settlers moving from the east coast of to seek territory further west. In 1890, US soldiers massacred over 150 Sioux at a place called **Wounded Knee Creek**, finally ending Native American resistance.

1890 Wounded Knee massacre

1903 First plane flight

1905 Theory of Relativity

1912 Race to South Pole

85 The first plane flight

Model of the *Wright Flyer*

This is a model of the '**Wright Flyer**', a plane built by American inventors **Orville and Wilbur Wright**. On December 17 1903, it became the **first plane to make a controlled, powered flight**. Piloted by Orville Wright, the plane flew for just over 20 seconds, above a beach in North Carolina.

86 The Theory of Relativity

In 1905, an office worker in Switzerland named **Albert Einstein** published four papers that changed the way scientists looked at the universe. Einstein's ideas, known together as the **Theory of Relativity,** were soon proved correct, redefining the laws of gravity. This photo of Einstein was taken in 1921, after he had become famous around the world.

Albert Einstein in 1921

87 Race to the South Pole

In January 1912, two teams of explorers raced to be the **first to reach the South Pole**. This picture was taken by the British team, led by **Captain Robert Falcon Scott**, after they had been beaten to the Pole by a Norwegian party led by **Roald Amundsen**. Tragically all Scott's team died on the march back.

88 The First World War

On June 28 1914, the heir to the Austrian throne, **Archduke Franz Ferdinand**, was killed by a Serbian student. Austria declared war on Serbia, and then more and more nations took sides. This led to the start of the **First World War**, a four year conflict that touched almost every country in the world. This poster was used by the British Army to **recruit new soldiers** to join the fighting.

British Army recruitment poster

89 The Western Front

Oppy Wood by John Nash

This **painting by John Nash** shows a section of the '**Western Front**' - lines of **trenches** along Northern France, where the two sides dug in to fight. During battle, soldiers scrambled from their trenches and charged at the enemy lines.

The World at War

In the 20th century, chaos erupted around the world, as nations fought in the First and Second World Wars, and then in a 'Cold War' of threats and distrust.

Statue of Lenin, St. Petersburg

90 The Russian Revolution

Russia suffered terribly in the First World War, in battle and at home, where food shortages led to starvation. In November 1917, a group of revolutionaries known as the '**Bolsheviks**' overthrew the ruler, Tsar Nicholas II, and seized power. This statue shows their leader, **Lenin**, who took Russia out of the war, and put workers in charge of factories. In 1922, Russia was renamed the **Union of Soviet Socialist Republics**, or Soviet Union.

1914-1918 First World War

1914 - 1945

1917 Russian Revolution

A British 'Spitfire' fighter plane

91 The Battle of Britain

In 1939, the **Second World War** erupted, between the **Axis Powers** (led by Nazi Germany under Adolf Hitler) and the **Allies** (including Britain, and later the Soviet Union and USA). In just a few months, the Germans captured most of Western Europe. In 1940, British planes – such as this **Spitfire** – fought off German attacks, ending Hitler's hopes of invading Britain.

92 D-Day

This photograph shows a scene from **June 6, 1944**, as around 150,000 Allied troops stormed the beaches of Normandy, in German-occupied France. It was the biggest invasion in history, code-named '**D-Day**'. The Allies captured the beaches, and continued to drive the German army back through Western Europe, while the Russians attacked the Germans from the East. On May 2, 1945, the **German army surrendered**.

British troops landing at Normandy on June 6, 1944

93 The Holocaust

As the War ended, the horrors of life under Nazi rule were revealed. At least 6 million Jews had been murdered in grim 'concentration camps' – a crime known as the **Holocaust**. In German-occupied areas, Jews were forced to wear yellow stars.

Photograph of a 'mushroom cloud' caused by an atomic bomb blast

94 Atomic warfare

Although the war in Europe ended in May 1945, fighting continued in the **Pacific**. On August 6, the USA dropped the first ever '**atomic bomb**' on the Japanese city of **Hiroshima**, killing 80,000 people. Three days later, another atomic bomb was dropped on the city of **Nagasaki**. This led to Japanese surrender, and the **end of the Second World War**.

1940 Battle of Britain

1944 D-Day

1941-1945 The Holocaust

1945 Atomic warfare

1947-1980 End of empires — from 1950 Cold War — 1962 Telstar 1 — 1960s Space Race

The flag of India

95 The end of empires

After the Second World War, people in **India** and ***Africa*** saw their chance to break free from European rulers. In India, a man named ***Mohandas Gandhi*** had led protests against British rule since the 1920s. Finally, on August 15, 1947, **India became independent**, with this new flag. By 1980, over 40 African nations had won independence too, after bitter struggles against their former rulers. **The age of great European empires was over.**

96 The Cold War

From around 1950, tensions between the USA and the communist Soviet Union led to a 40 year '**Cold War**' - a war of threats between the two sides. The city of **Berlin**, at the heart of the conflict, was divided by a **heavily guarded wall** separating areas controlled by different nations. This **sign** warned people they were leaving West Berlin to enter the communist East.

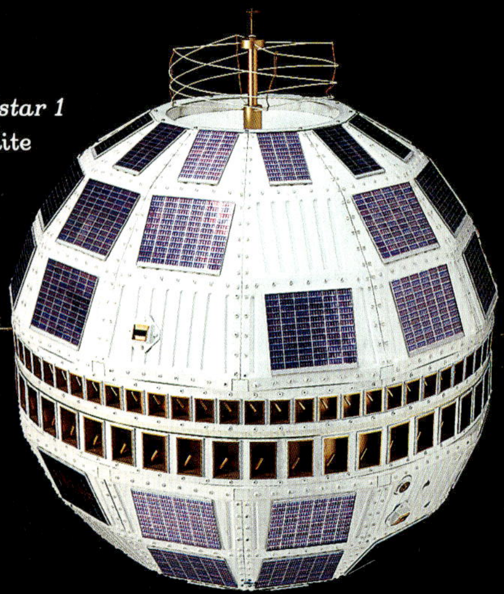

The *Telstar 1* satellite

97 Telstar 1

This 1m (3ft) high **satellite** - ***Telstar 1*** - was carried into space on a rocket on July 10, 1962. Fifteen hours later, it sent the **first ever live television pictures** across the ocean, from the USA to Europe. Telstar 1 also allowed the first long-distance phone calls, by receiving messages from Earth and instantly sending them back.

1989 World Wide Web

2000 Millennium celebrations

98 The Space Race

From around 1960, tensions between the USA and the Soviet Union led to a '**space race**', with both sides desperate to be the first to travel into space. In April 1961, Soviet 'cosmonaut' **Yuri Gagarin** became the **first person to orbit Earth**. Then, on July 20, 1969, two US 'astronauts' - **Buzz Aldrin** (shown here) and **Neil Armstrong** - became **the first men to walk on the Moon**.

Buzz Aldrin on the Moon, July 20, 1969

99 Computer revolution

A computer microprocessor

Computer technololgy developed rapidly in the second half of the 20th century. The invention of 'transistors', 'microchips' and then '**microprocessors**' (shown here) made computers faster, smaller and much more powerful. The **internet** was developed in the 1980s. In 1989, British scientist Tim Berners-Lee invented the '**World Wide Web**', which allowed people all over the world to use the internet.

100 Millennium celebrations

The 20th century ended with parties all around the world, to **celebrate the start of the year 2000**. Here, fireworks explode around the **Eiffel Tower**, in Paris, at midnight on December 31, 1999.

Index

Internet Links

For links to websites with videos about key figures and events, virtual tours of world heritage sites and zoomable images of priceless artifacts, go to the Usborne Quicklinks website at **www.usborne.com/quicklinks** and type in the title of this book. Please follow the internet safety guidelines at the Usborne Quicklinks website.

Acknowledgements

Every effort has been made to trace and acknowledge ownership of copyright. If any rights have been omitted, the publishers offer to rectify this in any future editions following notification. The publishers are grateful to the following individuals and organizations for their permission to reproduce material on the following pages:

COVER Spitfire © Michael Cole/Getty Images; Greek vase © Louvre, Paris, France / Bridgeman Images; Khmer statue © DeAgostini Picture Library/Scala, Florence; Aztec serpent © The Trustees of the British Museum; Napoleon © GL Archive / Alamy Stock Photo; Light bulb © Daniel Dempster Photography / Alamy Stock Photo.
PAGES 2-3 p2 t © Mary Evans/Glasshouse Images; m © The Trustees of the British Museum; b © British Museum / Universal History Archive/UIG / Bridgeman Images; p3 t © De Agostini Picture Library / M. Carrieri / Bridgeman Images; mr © Thaliastock / Mary Evans; ml © Werner Forman Archive; b © Photo Scala Florence.
PAGES 4-5 p4 tl © National Archaeological Museum, Athens, Greece / Bridgeman Images; tr © The Asahi Shimbun/Getty Images; bl © Werner Forman Archive; br © The Trustees of the British Museum; p5 tl © Werner Forman Archive/Jalapa Museum/ Vera Cruz; tr © Musée Guimet, Paris, France / Bridgeman Images; b © Werner Forman Archive.
PAGES 6-7 p6 t © Louvre, Paris, France / Bridgeman Images; m © De Agostini Picture Library / G. Dagli Orti / Bridgeman Images; b © Museo Archeologico Nazionale, Naples, Italy / Bridgeman Images; p7 tl © Tomb of Qin shi Huang Di, Xianyang, China / Bridgeman Images; tr © Werner Forman Archive; m © The Trustees of the British Museum; b © Byzantine Museum, Athens, Greece / Bridgeman Images.
PAGES 8-9 p8 t © Pictures from History / Bridgeman Images; m © San Vitale, Ravenna, Italy / Bridgeman Images; b © The Trustees of the British Museum; p9 t © 2017 Photo Scala, Florence; m © Bibliothèque des Arts Decoratifs, Paris, France / Archives Charmet / Bridgeman Images; b © Ivy Close Images / Alamy Stock Photo.
PAGES 10-11 p10 t © Peter Willi / Bridgeman Images; ml © The Print Collector/Heritage-Images/Scala, Florence; mr © Bonhams, London, UK / Bridgeman Images; b © Werner Forman Archive; p11 tl © Bibliothèque Municipale, Castres, France / Bridgeman Images; tr © National Museum of India, New Delhi, India / Bridgeman Images; b © DeAgostini Picture Library/Scala, Florence.
PAGES 12-13 p12 t © Musée de la Tapisserie, Bayeux, France / Bridgeman Images; ml © Werner Forman Archive; mr © Bibliothèque Nationale, Paris, France / Bridgeman Images; b © Peter Newark Military Pictures / Bridgeman Images; p13 t © The Stapleton Collection / Bridgeman Images; m © Bibliothèque Nationale, Paris, France / Bridgeman Images; b © National Archives, UK / Bridgeman Images.
PAGES 14-15 p14 t © Chartres Cathedral, Chartres, France / Bridgeman Images; bl © Bibliothèque Nationale, Paris, France / Bridgeman Images; br © Martin Wierink / Alamy Stock Photo; p15 t Private Collection / Bridgeman Images; ml © The Trustees of the British Museum; mr © Indianapolis Museum of Art, USA / Gift of Mr and Mrs Eli Lilly / Bridgeman Images; b Bildarchiv Steffens / Bridgeman Images.
PAGES 16-17 p16 tl © State Hermitage Museum, St. Petersburg, Russia / Bridgeman Images; tr © Museum der Stadt, Regensburg, Bavaria, Germany / Bridgeman Images; b © Science Museum, London, UK / Bridgeman Images; p17 tl © The Trustees of the British Museum; tr © De Agostini Picture Library / G. Dagli Orti / Bridgeman Images; m © Peter Horree / Alamy Stock Photo; b © Deco / Alamy Stock Photo.
PAGES 18-19 p18 t © British Library Board. All Rights Reserved / Bridgeman Images; ml © British Library Board. All Rights Reserved / Bridgeman Images; mr © Victoria & Albert Museum, London, UK / Bridgeman Images; b © Rafael Valls Gallery, London, UK / Bridgeman Images; p19 t © Kremlin Museums, Moscow, Russia / Bridgeman Images; m © Rischgitz/Getty Images; b © Brooklyn Museum of Art, New York, USA / Bridgeman Images.
PAGES 20-21 p20 t © Chateau de Versailles, France / Bridgeman Images; m © Private Collection / Bridgeman Images; b © 2017 DeAgostini Picture Library/Scala, Florence; p21 t © World History Archive / TopFoto; m © Private Collection / Bridgeman Images; b © Musée de la Ville de Paris, Musée Carnavalet, Paris, France / Bridgeman Images.
PAGES 22-23 p22 t © GL Archive / Alamy Stock Photo; m © British Library Board. All Rights Reserved / Bridgeman Images; b © ACORN 2 / Alamy Stock Photo; p23 t © INTERFOTO / Alamy Stock Photo; m © The Trustees of the British Museum; bl © De Agostini Picture Library / Bridgeman Images; br © National Media Museum, Bradford, West Yorkshire / Bridgeman Images.
PAGES 24-25 P24 t © Bibliothèque des Arts Decoratifs, Paris, France / Archives Charmet / Bridgeman Images; m © Natural History Museum, London, UK / Bridgeman Images; b © Leisa Tyler/LightRocket/Getty Images; p25 t © Civil War Archive / Bridgeman Images; m © Private Collection / Archives Charmet / Bridgeman Images; b © National Army Museum, London / Bridgeman Images.
PAGES 26-27 p26 t © Daniel Dempster Photography / Alamy Stock Photo; m © Rainer W. Schlegelmilch/Getty Images; b © Buffalo Bill Center of the West, Cody, Wyoming, U.S.A.; Gift of The New Hampshire Historical Society, NA.204.2; p27 t © Science & Society Picture Library/Getty Images; m © Pictorial Press Ltd / Alamy Stock Photo; b © English Photographer, (20th century) / Private Collection / The Stapleton Collection / Bridgeman Images.
PAGES 28-29 p28 t © Imperial War Museum, London, UK / Bridgeman Images; m © Oppy Wood, 1917. Evening, Nash, John Northcote (1893-1977) / Imperial War Museum, London, UK / Bridgeman Images; b © Matteo De Sanctis/Getty Images; p29 t © Michael Cole/Getty Images; m © Tallandier / Bridgeman Images; bl © Galerie Bilderwelt / Bridgeman Images; br © National Archives.
PAGES 30-31 P30 m © David Levenson / Alamy Stock Photo; b © Science & Society Picture Library/Getty Images; p31 t © Science & Society Picture Library /Getty Images; m © NASA; b © REUTERS / Alamy Stock Photo.

With thanks to Ruth King   Managing designer: Stephen Moncrieff

First published in 2017 by Usborne Publishing Ltd, Usborne House, 83-85 Saffron Hill, London EC1N 8RT, England. www.usborne.com